1001
Things to Spot
at
Christmas

Alex Frith

Illustrated by Teri Gower

Designed by Teri Gower and Nelupa Hussain
Edited by Anna Milbourne
Cover design by Helen Lee

Contents

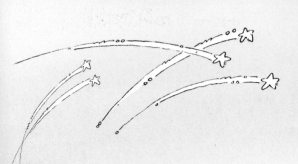

Things to spot

Preparing for Christmas is jolly hard work. Join Santa and his team of helpers as they set about making Christmas a magical holiday for everyone. Each scene in this book is full of Christmassy things for you to find and count. There are 1001 things to spot altogether.

Snowball fight!

8 dazed pixies

3 snow forts

8 spotted scarves

10 fir trees

5 snowmen

8 red elves

10 ice imps

8 yellow elves

3 snow cannons

7 catapults

Each little picture shows you what to look for in the big picture.

The number tells you how many of that thing you need to find.

This is Smudge the penguin. He's come to spend the winter with Santa and his hard-working helpers. Can you find him in every scene?

Christmas Land

4

 **5** elves chopping

 8 reindeer

 **4** snow boots

 5 Advent calendars

 **9** Christmas wishes

 1 Mrs. Claus

 **9** festive wreaths

 **10** mail pixies

 **7** elves on sleighs

Decorating the tree

6 snowy owls

7 hot drinks

10 silver stars

9 hearts

3 ladders

6

6 nutcracker men

7 snowy squirrels

10 pine cones

9 snowdrops

8 snowball pixies

Snowball fight!

5 snowmen

8

8 dazed pixies

3 snow forts

8 spotted scarves

10 fir trees

8 red elves

10 ice imps

8 yellow elves

3 snow cannons

7 catapults

Santa's workshop

9 dolls

10 teddy bears

8 red levers

7 robot hands

8 toymaker elves

5 oilcans

2 pie elves

10 yellow bows

8 striped balls

6 red cars

Winter games

8 flags

6 gnomes

1 musk ox

10 hoops

9 cheering fairies

12

5 frost monsters 7 racing sleds 9 snowsurfing elves 4 polar bears 9 hockey sticks

Christmas baking

5 smiling pans

8 cookie cutters

7 gingerbread men

9 sugar mice

8 pastry elves

7 white plates

9 festive pies

5 rolling pins

3 pixies with whisks

10 magic cakes

Midwinter ball

10 mugs of hot cocoa

6 elves dancing

7 fiddle players

8 snow geese

6 pixies skating

7 ice sculptures

9 masks

10 lanterns

7 merry mice

1 Jack Frost

Reindeer stables

2 fairy supervisors

7 reindeer dinners

6 pixies polishing

8 reindeer brushes

10 bags of magic dust

5 bottles of hoof oil

6 elf mechanics

9 buckets of water

7 paintbrushes

6 baby reindeer

Above the rooftops

4 green sleighs

6 singing cats

8 silver bells

1 town clock

10 purple presents

8 streetlights

10 present pixies

9 chimneys

8 strings of lights

7 shooting stars

Down the chimney

8 stockings

4 sleeping cats

3 sprigs of mistletoe

9 scampering mice

8 Christmas angels

22

9 candy canes

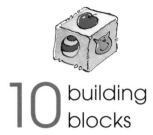

10 building blocks

5 carrots

10 cookies

9 fairy wands

Tropical Christmas

6 sandcastles

10 coconuts

3 boats with lights

2 lighthouses

10 palm trees

9 elves in swimsuits

10 fireworks

5 deck chairs

8 turtles

6 dolphins

Christmas feast

10 cranberry pies   6 yule logs   7 candles   10 party hats   4 Christmas cakes

8 pixies
singing

3 gnomes
eating pie

10 glasses of
fizzy pop

8 sugared
apples

9 party
poppers

Santa's day off

10 puzzle
books

6 socks for
Santa

4 dice

10 thank-you
letters

9 elves
dozing

 **8** plates of sandwiches

 **7** boxes of chocolates

 **9** pixies on skates

 **5** toy trains

 **1** snoozing Santa

Gifts for Santa

Every year after their Christmas feast, Santa's helpers give him gifts. Look back through the book and see if you can find and count all these gifts.

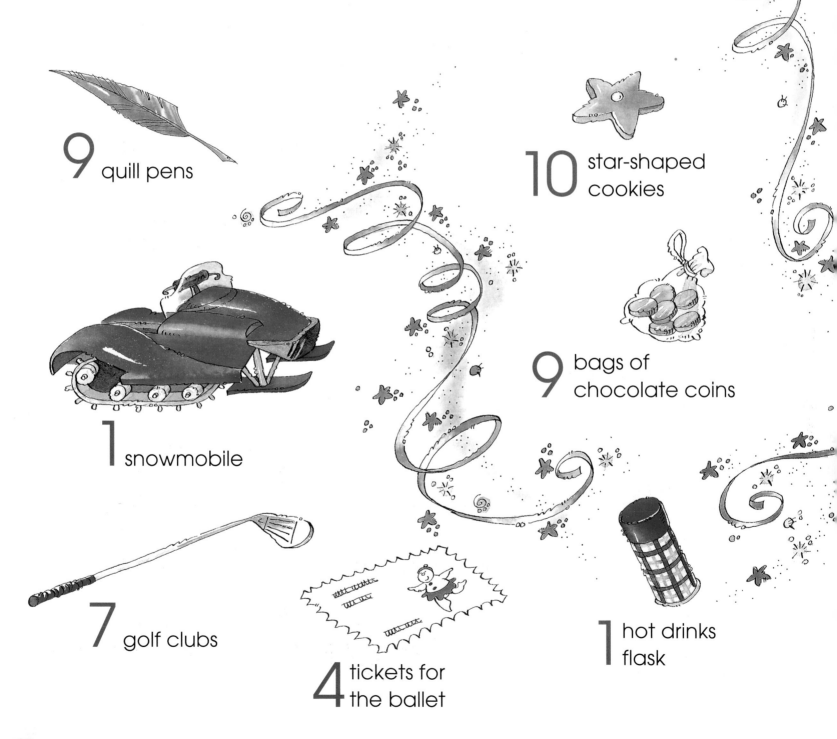

9 quill pens

10 star-shaped cookies

1 snowmobile

9 bags of chocolate coins

7 golf clubs

4 tickets for the ballet

1 hot drinks flask

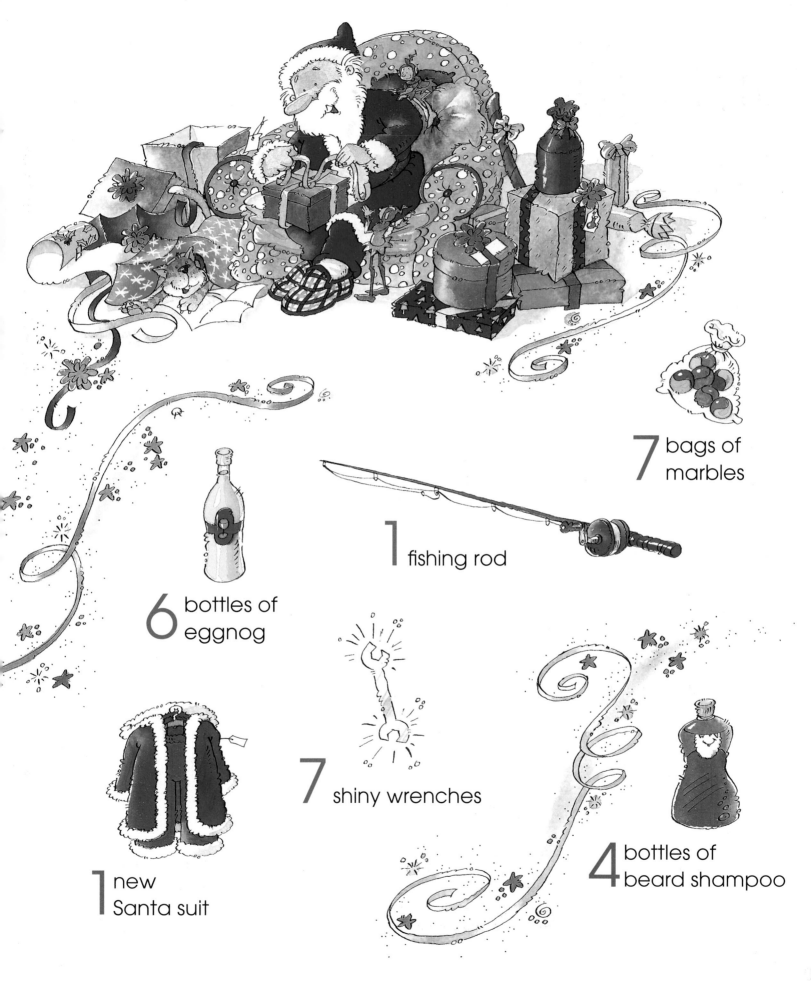

7 bags of marbles

1 fishing rod

6 bottles of eggnog

7 shiny wrenches

1 new Santa suit

4 bottles of beard shampoo

Answers

Did you spot all of Santa's gifts?
Here's where you can find them:

9 quill pens:
pages 4-5

10 star-shaped
cookies:
pages 14-15

1 snowmobile:
pages 10-11

9 bags of
chocolate coins:
pages 6-7

7 golf clubs:
pages 8-9

4 tickets for
the ballet:
pages 22-23

1 hot drinks flask:
pages 12-13

6 bottles of eggnog:
pages 16-17

1 fishing rod:
pages 24-25

7 bags of marbles:
pages 20-21

1 new Santa suit:
pages 28-29

7 shiny wrenches:
pages 18-19

4 bottles of
beard shampoo:
pages 26-27

First published in 2009 by Usborne Publishing Ltd.,
Usborne House, 83-85 Saffron Hill, London EC1N 8RT, England. www.usborne.co.uk
Copyright © 2009, Usborne Publishing Ltd. The name Usborne and the devices ♀ ⊕ are Trade Marks of Usborne Publishing Ltd.
All rights reserved. No part of this publication may be reproduced, stored in a retrieval system, or transmitted in any form
or by any means, electronic, mechanical, photocopying, recording or otherwise, without the prior permission of the publisher.
First published in America in 2009. UE. Printed in China.